Religions of
Ancient China

By HERBERT A. GILES, M.A., LL.D. (Aberd.)

*Professor of Chinese at the University of Cambridge,
Author of "Historic China," "A History
of Chinese Literature," "China and
the Chinese," etc., etc.*

First Published 1906 by Constable and Company Ltd., London.

This book has been published by:

Contact: sales@nuvisionpublications.com

URL: http://www.nuvisionpublications.com

Publishing Date: 2008

ISBN# 1-59547-717-9

Please see our website for several books created for education, research and entertainment.

Specializing in rare, out-of-print books still in demand.

NuVision Publications, LLC is dedicated to bringing new life to rare, historic, and formerly out-of-print books. Most re-print publishers simply photocopy, or scan and print the pages from the original book, which can make the book hard to read as most re-print books are 100+ years old. It is our policy to take the time to convert the original faded, sometimes blotched text into crisp, clear digital text. All of our printed books have been completely reformatted to be easy to read and enjoy.

Please note that we do not correct out-of-date facts or grammar-type errors that were in the original book. We do our best to retain the original composition of the text, the way the author intended it.

NuVision Publications, LLC
Sioux Falls, SD USA

Contents

CHAPTER I

THE ANCIENT FAITH

Philosophical Theory of the Universe.--The problem of the universe has never offered the slightest difficulty to Chinese philosophers. Before the beginning of all things, there was Nothing. In the lapse of ages Nothing coalesced into Unity, the Great Monad. After more ages, the Great Monad separated into Duality, the Male and Female Principles in nature; and then, by a process of biogenesis, the visible universe was produced.

Popular Cosmogeny.--An addition, however, to this simple system had to be made, in deference to, and on a plane with, the intelligence of the masses. According to this, the Male and Female Principles were each subdivided into Greater and Lesser, and then from the interaction of these four agencies a being, named P'an Ku, came into existence. He seems to have come into life endowed with perfect knowledge, and his function was to set the economy of the universe in order. He is often depicted as wielding a huge adze, and engaged in constructing the world. With his death the details of creation began. His breath became the wind; his voice, the thunder; his left eye, the sun; his right eye, the moon; his blood flowed in rivers; his hair grew into trees and plants; his flesh became the soil; his sweat descended as rain; while the parasites which infested his body were the origin of the human race.

Recognition and Worship of Spirits.--Early Chinese writers tell us that Fu Hsi, B.C. 2953-2838, was the first Emperor to organize sacrifices to, and worship of, spirits. In this he was followed by the Yellow Emperor, B.C. 2698-2598, who built a temple for the worship of God, in which incense was used, and first sacrificed to the Mountains and Rivers. He is also said to have established the worship of the sun, moon, and five planets, and to have elaborated the ceremonial of ancestral worship.

God the Father, Earth the Mother.--The Yellow Emperor was followed by the Emperor Shao Hao, B.C. 2598-2514, "who instituted the music of the Great Abyss in order to bring spirits and men into harmony." Then came the Emperor Chuan Hsu, B.C. 2514-2436, of whom it is said that he appointed an officer "to preside over the worship of God and Earth, in order to form a link between the spirits and man," and also "caused music to be played for the enjoyment of God." **God Worshipped with musle and dancing--** Music, by the way, is said to have been introduced into worship in imitation of thunder, and was therefore supposed to be pleasing to the Almighty. After him followed the Emperor Ti K'u, B.C. 2436-2366, who dabbled in astronomy, and "came to a knowledge of spiritual beings, which he respectfully worshipped." The Emperor Yao, B.C. 2357-2255, built a temple for the worship of God, and also caused dances to be performed for the enjoyment of God on occasions of special sacrifice and communication with the spiritual world. After him, we reach the Emperor Shun, B.C. 2255-2205, in whose favour Yao abdicated.

Additional Deities.--Before, however, Shun ventured to mount the throne, he consulted the stars, in order to find out if the unseen Powers were favourable to his elevation; and on receiving a satisfactory reply, "he proceeded to sacrifice to God, to the Six Honoured Ones (unknown), to the Mountains and Rivers, and to Spirits in general. . . . In the second month of the year, he made a tour of inspection eastwards, as far as Mount T'ai (in modern Shantung), where he presented a burnt offering to God, and sacrificed to the Mountains and Rivers."

God punishes the wicked and rewards the good.--The Great Yu, who drained the empire, and came to the throne in B.C. 2205 as first Emperor of the Hsia dynasty, followed in the lines of his pious predecessors. But the Emperor K'ung Chia, B.C. 1879-1848, who at first had treated the Spirits with all due reverence, fell into evil ways, and was abandoned by God. This was the beginning of the end. In B.C. 1766 T'ang the Completer, founder of the Shang dynasty, set to work to overthrow Chieh Kuei, the last ruler of the Hsia dynasty. He began by sacrificing to Almighty God, and asked for a blessing on his undertaking. And in his subsequent proclamation to the empire, he spoke of that God as follows: "God has given to every man a conscience; and if all men acted in accordance with its dictates, they would not stray from the right path. . . . The way of God is to bless the good and punish the bad. He has sent down calamities on the House of Hsia, to make manifest its crimes."

God manifests displeasure.--In B.C. 1637 the Emperor T'ai Mou succeeded. His reign was marked by the supernatural appearance in the palace of two mulberry-trees, which in a single night grew to such a size that they could hardly be spanned by two hands. The Emperor was terrified; whereupon a Minister said, "No prodigy is a match for virtue. Your Majesty's government is no doubt at fault, and some reform of conduct is necessary." Accordingly, the Emperor began to act more circumspectly; after which the mulberry-trees soon withered and died.

Revelation in a dream.--The Emperor Wu Ting, B.C. 1324-1264, began his reign by not speaking for three years, leaving all State affairs to be decided by his Prime Minister, while he himself gained experience. Later on, the features of a sage were revealed to him in a dream; and on waking, he caused a portrait of the apparition to be prepared and circulated throughout the empire. The sage was found, and for a long time aided the Emperor in the right administration of government. On the occasion of a sacrifice, a pheasant perched upon the handle of the great sacrificial tripod, and crowed, at which the Emperor was much alarmed. "Be not afraid," cried a Minister; "but begin by reforming your government. God looks down upon mortals, and in accordance with their deserts grants them many years or few. God does not shorten men's lives; they do that themselves. Some are wanting in virtue, and will not acknowledge their transgressions; only when God chastens them do they cry, What are we to do?"

Anthropomorphism and Fetishism.--One of the last Emperors of the Shang dynasty, Wu I, who reigned B.C. 1198-1194, even went so far as "to make an image in human form, which he called God. With this image he used to play at dice, causing some one to throw for the image; and if 'God' lost, he would overwhelm the image with insult. He also made a bag of leather, which he filled with blood and hung up. Then he would shoot at it, saying that he was shooting God. By and by, when he was out hunting, he was struck down by a violent thunderclap, and killed."

God indignant.--Finally, when the Shang dynasty sank into the lowest depths of moral abasement, King Wu, who charged himself with its overthrow, and who subsequently became the first sovereign of the Chou dynasty, offered sacrifices to Almighty God, and also to Mother Earth. "The King of Shang," he said in his address to the high officers who collected around him, "does not reverence God above, and inflicts calamities on the people below. Almighty God is moved with indignation." On the day of the final battle he declared that he was acting in the matter of punishment merely as the instrument of God; and after his great victory and the establishment of his own line, it was to God that he rendered thanks.

No Devil, No Hell.--In this primitive monotheism, of which only scanty, but no doubt genuine, records remain, no place was found for any being such as the Buddhist Mara or the Devil of the Old and New Testaments. God inflicted His own punishments by visiting calamities on mankind, just as He bestowed His own rewards by sending bounteous harvests in due season. Evil spirits were a later invention, and their operations were even then confined chiefly to tearing people's hearts out, and so forth, for their own particular pleasure; we certainly meet no cases of evil spirits wishing to undermine man's allegiance to God, or desiring to make people wicked in order to secure their everlasting punishment. The vision of Purgatory, with all its horrid tortures, was introduced into China by Buddhism, and was subsequently annexed by the Taoists, some time between the third and sixth centuries A.D.

Chinese Terms for God.--Before passing to the firmer ground, historically speaking, of the Chou dynasty, it may be as well to state here that there are two terms in ancient Chinese literature which seem to be used indiscriminately for God. One is *T'ien*, which has come to include the material heavens, the sky; and the other is *Shang Ti*, which has come to include the spirits of deceased Emperors. These two terms appear simultaneously, so to speak, in the earliest documents which have come down to us, dating back to something like the twentieth century before Christ. Priority, however, belongs beyond all doubt to *T'ien*, which it would have been more natural to find meaning, first the visible heavens, and secondly the Deity, whose existence beyond the sky would be inferred from such phenomena as lightning, thunder, wind, and rain. But the process appears to have been the other way, so far at any rate as the written language is concerned. The Chinese script, when it first came into existence, was purely pictorial, and confined to visible objects which were comparatively easy to depict. There does not seem to have been any attempt to draw a picture of the sky. On the other hand, the character *T'ien* was just such a representation of a human being as would be expected from the hand of a prehistoric artist; and under this unmistakable shape the character appears on bells and tripods, as seen in collections of inscriptions, so late as the sixth and seventh centuries B.C., after which the head is flattered to a line, and the arms are raised until they form another line parallel to that of the head.

THE ANCIENT FAITH

Extracts from the *Hsiao-t'ang-chi-ku-lu*, Pt. I, pp. 12 *verso*, 20 *verso*, and Pt. II, p. 25 *recto*.

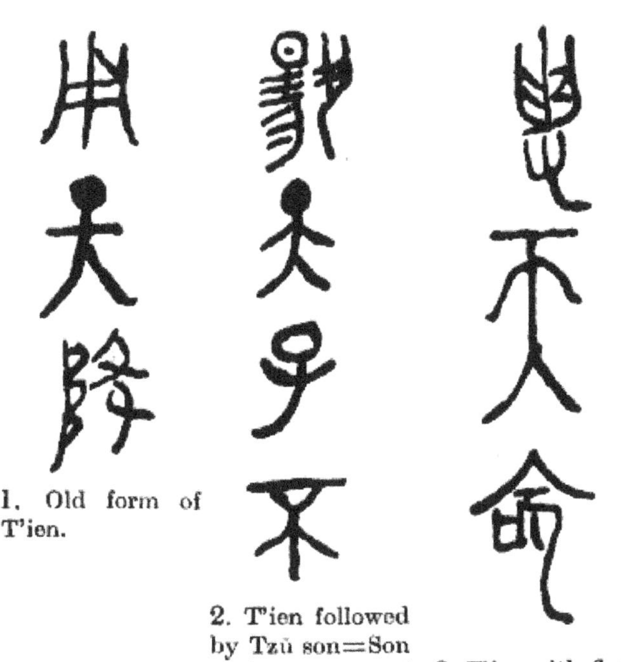

1. Old form of T'ien.

2. T'ien followed by Tzŭ son=Son of God, or Son of Heaven.

3. T'ien with flattened head.

4. Modern form of T'ien.

Distinction between T'ien and Shang Ti.--The term *Shang Ti* means literally Supreme Ruler. It is not quite so vague as *T'ien*, which seems to be more of an abstraction, while *Shang Ti* is a genuinely personal God. Reference to *T'ien* is usually associated with fate or destiny, calamities, blessings, prayers for help, etc. The commandments of *T'ien* are hard to obey; He is compassionate, to be feared, unjust, and cruel. *Shang Ti* lives in heaven, walks, leaves tracks on the ground, enjoys the sweet savour of sacrifice, approves or disapproves of conduct, deals with rewards and punishments in a more particular way, and comes more actually into touch with the human race.

Thus *Shang Ti* would be the God who walked in the garden in the cool of the day, the God who smelled the sweet savour of Noah's sacrifice, and the God who allowed Moses to see His back. *T'ien* would be the God of Gods of the Psalms, whose mercy endureth for ever; the everlasting God of Isaiah, who fainteth not, neither is weary.

Roman Catholic Dissensions.--These two, in fact, were the very terms favoured by the early Jesuit missionaries to China, though not with the limitations above suggested, as fit the proper renderings for God; and of the two terms the great Manchu Emperor K'ang Hsi chose *T'ien*. It has been thought that the conversion of China to Christianity under the guiding influence of the Jesuits would soon have become an accomplished fact, but for the ignorant opposition to the use of these terms by the Franciscans and Dominicans, who referred this question, among others, to the Pope. In 1704 Clement XI published a bull declaring that the Chinese equivalent for God was *T'ien Chu*=Lord of Heaven; and such it has continued to be ever since, so far as the Roman Catholic church is concerned, in spite of the fact that *T'ien Chu* was a name given at the close of the third century B.C. to one of the Eight Spirits.

The two Terms are One.--That the two terms refer in Chinese thought to one and the same Being, though possibly with differing attributes, even down to modern times, may be seen from the account of a dream by the Emperor Yung Lo, A.D. 1403-1425, in which His Majesty relates that an angel appeared to him, with a message from *Shang Ti*; upon which the Emperor remarked, "Is not this a command from *T'ien*?" A comparison might perhaps be instituted with the use of "God" and "Jehovah" in the Bible. At the same time it must be noted that this view was not suggested by the Emperor K'ang Hsi, who fixed upon *T'ien* as the appropriate term. It is probable that, vigorous Confucianist as he was, he was anxious to appear on the side rather of an abstract than of a personal Deity, and that he was repelled by the overwrought anthropomorphism of the Christian God. His conversion was said to have been very near at times; we read, however, that, when hard pressed by the missionaries to accept baptism, "he always excused himself by saying that he worshipped the same God as the Christians."

God in the "Odes."--The Chou dynasty lasted from B.C. 1122 to B.C. 255. It was China's feudal age, when the empire, then included between latitude 34-40 and longitude 109-118, was split up into a number of vassal States, which owned allegiance to a suzerain State. And it is to the earlier centuries of the Chou dynasty that must be attributed the composition of a large number of ballads of various kinds, ultimately collected and edited by Confucius, and now known as the *Odes*. **He is Anthropomorphic and Personal--** From these *Odes* it is abundantly clear that the Chinese people continued to hold, more clearly and more firmly than ever, a deep-seated belief in the existence of an anthropomorphic and personal God, whose one care was the welfare of the human race:--

There is Almighty God;
Does He hate any one?

He reigns in glory.--The soul of King Wen, father of the King Wu below, and posthumously raised by his son to royal rank, is represented as enjoying happiness in a state beyond the grave:--

King Wen is on high,
In glory in heaven.
His comings and his goings
Are to and from the presence of God.

He is a Spirit.--Sometimes in the *Odes* there is a hint that God, in spite of His anthropomorphic semblance, is a spirit:--

The doings of God
Have neither sound nor smell.

Spiritual Beings.--Spirits were certainly supposed to move freely among mortals:--

Do not say, This place is not public;
No one can see me here.
The approaches of spiritual Beings
Cannot be calculated beforehand;
But on no account should they be ignored.

The God of Battle.--In the hour of battle the God of ancient China was as much a participator in the fight as the God of Israel in the Old Testament:--

God is on your side!

was the cry which stimulated King Wu to break down the opposing ranks of Shang. To King Wu's father, and others, direct communications had previously been made from heaven, with a view to the regeneration of the empire:--

The dynasties of Hsia and Shang
Had not satisfied God with their government;
So throughout the various States
He sought and considered

For a State on which He might confer the rule.

God said to King Wen,
I am pleased with your conspicuous virtue,
Without noise and without display,
Without heat and without change,
Without consciousness of effort,
Following the pattern of God.

God said to King Wen,
Take measures against hostile States,
Along with your brethren,
Get ready your grappling-irons,
And your engines of assault,
To attack the walls of Ts'ung.

God sends Famine.--The *Ode* from which the following extract is taken carries us back to the ninth century B.C., at the time of a prolonged and disastrous drought:--

Glorious was the Milky Way,
Revolving brightly in the sky,
When the king said, Alas!
What crime have my people committed now,
That God sends down death and disorder,
And famine comes upon us again?
There is no spirit to whom I have not sacrificed;
There is no victim that I have grudged;
Our sacrificial symbols are all used up;--
How is it that I am not heard?

The Confucian Criterion.--The keystone of the Confucian philosophy, that man is born good, will be found in the following lines:--

How mighty is God!
How clothed in majesty is God,
And how unsearchable are His judgments!
God gives birth to the people,
But their natures are not constant;
All have the same beginning,
But few have the same end.

God, however, is not held responsible for the sufferings of mankind. King Wen, in an address to the last tyrant of the House of Shang, says plainly,

It is not God who has caused this evil time,
But it is you who have strayed from the old paths.

The Associate of God.--Worshipped on certain occasions as the Associate of God, and often summoned to aid in hours of distress or danger, was a personage known as Hou Chi, said to have been the original ancestor of the House of Chou. **Parthenogenesis--** His story, sufficiently told in the *Odes*, is curious for several reasons, and especially for an instance in Chinese literature, which, in the absence of any known husband, comes near suggesting the much-vexed question of parthenogenesis:--

She who first gave birth to our people
Was the lady Chiang Yuan.
How did she give birth to them?
She offered up a sacrifice
That she might not be childless;
Then she trod in a footprint of God's, and conceived,
The great and blessed one,
Pregnant with a new birth to be,
And brought forth and nourished
Him who was Hou Chi.

When she had fulfilled her months,
Her firstborn came forth like a lamb.
There was no bursting, no rending,
No injury, no hurt,
In order to emphasise his divinity.
Did not God give her comfort?
Had He not accepted her sacrifice,
So that thus easily she brought forth her son?

He was exposed in a narrow lane,
But sheep and oxen protected and suckled him;
He was exposed in a wide forest,
But woodcutters found him;
He was exposed on cold ice,
But birds covered him with their wings.

Apotheosis of Hou Chi.--And so he grew to man's estate, and taught the people husbandry, with a success that has never been rivalled. Consequently, he was deified, and during several centuries of the Chou dynasty was united in worship with God:--

O wise Hou Chi,
Fit Associate of our God,
Founder of our race,
There is none greater than thou!
Thou gavest us wheat and barley,
Which God appointed for our nourishment,

And without distinction of territory,
Didst inculcate the virtues over our vast dominions.

Other Deities.--During the long period covered by the Chou dynasty, various other deities, of more or less importance, were called into existence.

The patriarchal Emperor Shen Nung, B.C. 2838-2698, who had taught his people to till the ground and eat of the fruits of their labour, was deified as the tutelary genius of agriculture:--

That my fields are in such good condition
Is matter of joy to my husbandmen.
With lutes, and with drums beating,
We will invoke the Father of Husbandry,
And pray for sweet rain,
To increase the produce of our millet fields,
And to bless my men and their wives.

There were also sacrifices to the Father of War, whoever he may have been; to the Spirits of Wind, Rain, and Fire; and even to a deity who watched over the welfare of silkworms. Since those days, the number of spiritual beings who receive worship from the Chinese, some in one part of the empire, some in another, has increased enormously. A single work, published in 1640, gives notices of no fewer than eight hundred divinities.

Superstitions.--During the period under consideration, all kinds of superstition prevailed; among others, that of referring to the rainbow. The rainbow was believed by the vulgar to be an emanation from an enormous oyster away in the great ocean which surrounded the world, i.e. China. Philosophers held it to be the result of undue proportions in the mixture of the two cosmogonical principles which when properly blended produce the harmony of nature. By both parties it was considered to be an inauspicious manifestation, and merely to point at it would produce a sore on the hand.

Supernatural Manifestations.--Several events of a supernatural character are recorded as having taken place under the Chou dynasty. In B.C. 756, one of the feudal Dukes saw a vision of a yellow serpent which descended from heaven and laid its head on the slope of a mountain. The Duke spoke of this to his astrologer, who said, "It is a manifestation of God; sacrifice to it."

In B.C. 747, another Duke found on a mountain a being in the semblance of a stone. Sacrifices were at once offered, and the stone was deified, and received regular worship from that time forward.

In B.C. 659, a third Duke was in a trance for five days, when he saw a vision of God, and received from Him instructions as to matters then pressing. For many generations afterwards the story ran that the Duke had been up to Heaven. This became a favourite theme for romancers. It is stated in the biography of a certain Feng Po that "one night he saw the gate of heaven open, and beheld exceeding glory within, which shone into his courtyard."

The following story is told by Huai-nan Tzu (d. B.C. 122):--"Once when the Duke of Lu-yang was at war with the Han State, and sunset drew near while a battle was still fiercely raging, the Duke held up his spear and shook it at the sun, which forthwith went back three zodiacal signs."

Only the Emperor worships God and Earth.--From the records of this period we can also see how jealously the worship of God and Earth was reserved for the Emperor alone.

In B.C. 651, Duke Huan of the Ch'i State, one of the feudal nobles to be mentioned later on, wished to signalise his accession to the post of doyen or leader of the vassal States by offering the great sacrifices to God and to Earth. He was, however, dissuaded from this by a wise Minister, who pointed out that only those could perform these ceremonies who had personally received the Imperial mandate from God.

This same Minister is said to be responsible for the following utterance:--

"Duke Huan asked Kuan Chang, saying, To what should a prince attach the highest importance? To God, replied the Minister; at which Duke Huan gazed upwards to the sky. The God I mean, continued Kuan Chung, is not the illimitable blue above. A true prince makes the people his God."

Sacrifices.--Much has been recorded by the Chinese on the subject of sacrifice,--more indeed than can be easily condensed into a small compass. First of all, there were the great sacrifices to God and to Earth, at the winter and summer solstices respectively, which were reserved for the Son of Heaven alone. Besides what may be called private sacrifices, the Emperor sacrificed also to the four quarters, and to the mountains and rivers of the empire; while the feudal nobles sacrificed each to his own quarter, and to the mountains and rivers of his own domain. The victim offered by the Emperor on a blazing pile of wood was an ox of one colour, always a young animal; a feudal noble would use any fatted ox; and a petty official a sheep or a pig. When sacrificing to the spirits of the land and of grain, the Son of Heaven used a bull, a ram, and a boar; the feudal nobles only a ram and a boar; and the common people, scallions and eggs in spring, wheat and fish in summer, millet and a sucking-pig in autumn, and unhulled rice and a goose in winter. If there was anything infelicitous about the victim intended for God, it was used for Hou Chi. The victim intended for God required to be kept in a clean stall for three months; that for Hou Chi simply required to be perfect in its parts. This was the way in which they distinguished between heavenly and earthly spirits.

In primeval times, we are told, sacrifices consisted of meat and drink, the latter being the "mysterious liquid," water, for which wine was substituted later on. The ancients roasted millet and pieces of pork; they made a hole in the ground and scooped the water from it with their two hands, beating upon an earthen drum with a clay drumstick. Thus they expressed their reverence for spiritual beings.

"Sacrifices," according to the *Book of Rites* (Legge's translation), "should not be frequently repeated. Such frequency is an indication of importunateness; and importunateness is inconsistent with reverence. Nor should they be at distant intervals. Such infrequency is indicative of indifference; and indifference leads to forgetting them altogether. Therefore the superior man, in harmony with the course of Nature, offers the sacrifices of spring and autumn. When he treads on the dew which has descended as hoar-frost he cannot help a feeling of sadness, which arises in his mind, and which cannot be ascribed to the cold. In spring, when he treads on the ground, wet with the rains and dews that have fallen heavily, he cannot avoid being moved by a feeling as if he were seeing his departed friends. We meet the approach of our friends with music, and escort them away with sadness, and hence at the sacrifice in spring we use music, but not at the sacrifice in autumn."

"Sacrifice is not a thing coming to a man from without; it issues from within him, and has its birth in his heart. When the heart is deeply moved, expression is given to it by ceremonies; and hence, only men of ability and virtue can give complete exhibition to the idea of sacrifice." It was in this sense that Confucius warned his followers not to sacrifice to spirits which did not belong to them, i.e. to other than those of their own immediate ancestors. To do otherwise would raise a suspicion of ulterior motives.

Ancestral Worship.--For the purpose of ancestral worship, which had been practised from the earliest ages, the Emperor had seven shrines, each with its altar representing various forefathers; and at all of these a sacrifice was offered every month. Feudal nobles could have only five sets of these, and the various officials three or fewer, on a descending scale in proportion to their rank. Petty officers and the people generally had no ancestral shrine, but worshipped the shades of their forefathers as best they could in their houses and cottages.

For three days before sacrificing to ancestors, a strict vigil and purification was maintained, and by the end of that time, from sheer concentration of thought, the mourner was able to see the spirits of the departed; and at the sacrifice next day seemed to hear their very movements, and even the murmur of their sighs.

The object of the ceremony was to bring down the spirits from above, together with the shades of ancestors, and thus to secure the blessing of God; at the same time to please the souls of the departed, and to create a link between the living and the dead.

"The object in sacrifices is not to pray; the time should not be hastened on; a great apparatus is not required; ornamental details are not to be approved; the victims need not be fat and large (cf. Horace, Od. III, 23; *Immunis aram*, etc.); a profusion of the other offerings is not to be admired." There must, however, be no parsimony. A high official, well able to afford better things, was justly blamed for having sacrificed to the manes of his father a sucking-pig which did not fill the dish.

Religious Dances.--"The various dances displayed the gravity of the performers, but did not awaken the emotion of delight. The ancestral temple produced the impression of majesty, but did not dispose one to rest on it. Its vessels might be employed, but could not be conveniently used for any other purpose. The idea which leads to intercourse with spiritual Beings is not interchangeable with that which finds its realisation in rest and pleasure."

Priestcraft.--From the ceremonial of ancestor worship the thin end of the wedge of priestcraft was rigorously excluded. "For the words of prayer and blessing and those of benediction to be kept hidden away by the officers of prayer of the ancestral temple, and by the sorcerers and recorders, is a violation of the rules of propriety. This may be called keeping in a state of darkness."

Confucius sums up the value of sacrifices in the following words. "By their great sacrificial ceremonies the ancients served God; by their ceremonies in the ancestral temple they worshipped their forefathers. He who should understand the great sacrificial ceremonies, and the meaning of the ceremonies in the ancestral temple, would find it as easy to govern the empire as to look upon the palm of his hand."

Filial Piety.--Intimately connected with ancestral worship is the practice of filial piety; it is in fact on filial piety that ancestral worship is dependent for its existence. In early ages, sons sacrificed to the manes of their parents and ancestors generally, in order to afford some mysterious pleasure to the disembodied spirits. There was then no idea of propitiation, of benefits to ensue. In later times, the character of the sacrifice underwent a change, until a sentiment of *do ut des* became the real mainspring of the ceremony. Meanwhile, Confucius had complained that the filial piety of his day only meant the support of parents. "But," argued the Sage, "we support our dogs and our horses; without reverence, what is there to distinguish one from the other?" He affirmed that children who would be accounted filial should give their parents no cause of anxiety beyond such anxiety as might be occasioned by ill-health. Filial piety, he said again, did not consist in relieving the parents of toil, or in setting before them wine and food; it did consist in serving them while alive according to the established rules, in burying them when dead according to the established rules, and in sacrificing to them after death, also according to the established rules. In another passage Confucius declared that filial piety consists in carrying on the aims of our forefathers, which really amounts to serving the dead as they would have been served if alive.

Divination.--Divination seems to have been practised in China from the earliest ages. The implements used were the shell of the tortoise, spiritualised by the long life of its occupant, and the stalks of a kind of grass, to which also spiritual powers had for some reason or other been attributed. These were the methods, we are told, by which the ancient Kings made their people revere spirits, obey the law, and settle all their doubts. God gave these spiritual boons to mankind, and the sages took advantage of them. "To explore what is complex, to search out what is hidden, to hook up what lies deep, and to reach to what is distant, thereby determining the issues for good or ill of all events under the sky, and making all men full of strenuous endeavour, there are no agencies greater than those of the stalks and the tortoise shell."

In B.C. 2224, when the Emperor Shun wished to associate the Great Yu with him in the government, the latter begged that recourse might be had to divination, in order to discover the most suitable among the Ministers for this exalted position. The Emperor refused, saying that his choice had already been confirmed by the body of Ministers. "The spirits too have signified their assent, the tortoise and grass having both concurred. Divination, when fortunate, may not be repeated."

Sincerity, on which Confucius lays such especial stress, is closely associated with success in divination. "Sincerity is of God; cultivation of sincerity is of man. He who is naturally sincere is he who hits his mark without effort, and without thinking apprehends. He easily keeps to the golden mean; he is inspired. He who cultivates sincerity is he who chooses what is good and holds fast to it.

"It is characteristic of the most entire sincerity to be able to foreknow. When a State or a family is about to flourish, there are sure to be happy omens; and when it is about to perish, there are sure to be unpropitious omens. The events portended are set forth by the divining-grass and the tortoise. When calamity or good fortune may be about to come, the evil or the good will be foreknown by the perfectly sincere man, who may therefore be compared with a spirit."

The tortoise and the grass have long since disappeared as instruments of divination, which is now carried on by means of lots drawn from a vase, with answers attached; by planchette; and by the *chiao*. The last consists of two pieces of wood, anciently of stone, in the shape of the two halves of a kidney bean. These are thrown into the air before the altar in a temple,--Buddhist or Taoist, it matters nothing, --with the following results. Two convex sides uppermost mean a response indifferently good; two flat sides mean negative and bad; one convex and one flat side mean that the prayer will be granted. This form of divination, though widely practised at the present day, is by no means of recent date. It was common in the Ch'u State, which was destroyed B.C. 300, after four hundred and twenty years of existence.

CHAPTER II

CONFUCIANISM

Attitude of Confucius.--Under the influence of Confucius, B.C. 551-479, the old order of things began to undergo a change. The Sage's attitude of mind towards religion was one of a benevolent agnosticism, as summed up in his famous utterance, "Respect the spirits, but keep them at a distance." That he fully recognised the existence of a spirit world, though admitting that he knew nothing about it, is manifest from the following remarks of his:--

"How abundantly do spiritual beings display the powers that belong to them! We look for, but do not see them; we listen for, but do not hear them; yet they enter into all things, and there is nothing without them. They cause all the people in the empire to fast and purify themselves, and array themselves in their richest dresses, in order to attend at their sacrifices. Then, like overflowing water, they seem to be over the heads, and on the right and left, of their worshippers."

He believed that he himself was, at any rate to some extent, a prophet of God, as witness his remarks when in danger from the people of K'uang:--

"After the death of King Wen, was not wisdom lodged in me? If God were to destroy this wisdom, future generations could not possess it. So long as God does not destroy this wisdom, what can the people of K'uang do to me?"

Again, when Confucius cried, "Alas! there is no one that knows me," and a disciple asked what was meant, he replied, "I do not murmur against God. I do not mumble against man. My studies lie low, and my penetration lies high. But there is God; He knows me."

We know that Confucius fasted, and we know that "he sacrificed to the spirits as though the spirits were present;" it is even stated that "when a friend sent him a present, though it might be a carriage and horses, unless it were flesh which had been used in sacrifice, he did not bow." He declared that for a person in mourning food and music were without flavour and charm; and whenever he saw anyone approaching who was in mourning dress, even though younger than himself, he would immediately rise from his seat. He believed in destiny; he was superstitious, changing colour at a squall or at a clap of thunder; and he even countenanced the ceremonies performed by villagers when driving out evil spirits from their dwellings. He protested against any attempt to impose on God. He said that "he who offends against God has none to whom he can pray;" and when in an hour of sickness a disciple asked to be allowed to pray for him, he replied, "My praying has been for a long time." Yet he declined to speak to his disciples of God, of spiritual beings or even of death and a hereafter, holding that life and its problems were alone sufficient to tax the energies of the human race. While not altogether ignoring man's duty towards God, he subordinated it in every way to man's duty towards his neighbour. He also did much towards weakening the personality of God, for whom he invariably used *T'ien*, never *Shang Ti*, regarding Him evidently more as an abstraction than as a living sentient Being, with the physical attributes of man. Confucianism is therefore entirely a system of morality, and not a religion.

It is also a curious fact that throughout the *Spring and Autumn,* or Annals of the State of Lu, which extend from B.C. 722 to B.C. 484, there is no allusion of any kind to the interposition of God in human affairs, although a variety of natural phenomena are recorded, such as have always been regarded by primitive peoples as the direct acts of an angered or benevolent Deity. Lu was the State in which Confucius was born, and its annals were compiled by the Sage himself; and throughout these Annals the term God is never used except in connection with the word "King," where it always has the sense of "by the grace of God," and once where the suzerain is spoken of as "the Son of God," or, as we usually phrase it, "the Son of Heaven."

How to bring rain.--In the famous Commentary by Tso-ch'iu Ming on the *Spring and Autumn,* which imparts a human interest to the bald entries set against each year of these annals, there are several allusions to the Supreme Being. For instance, at a time of great drought the Duke of Lu wished, in accordance with custom, to burn a witch and a person in the last stage of consumption; the latter being sometimes exposed in the sun so as to excite the compassion of God, who would then cause rain to fall. A Minister vigorously protested against this superstition, pointing out that the proper way to meet a drought would be to reduce the quantity of food consumed, and to practise rigid economy in all things. "What have these creatures to do with the matter?" he asked. "If God had wished to put them to death, He had better not have given them life. If they can really produce drought, to burn them will only increase the calamity." The Duke accordingly desisted; and although there was a famine, it is said to have been less severe than usual.

In B.C. 523 there was a comet. A Minister said, "This broom-star sweeps away the old, and brings in the new. The doings of God are constantly attended by such appearances."

Under B.C. 532 we have the record of a stone speaking. The Marquis of Lu enquired of his chief musician if this was a fact, and received the following answer: "Stones cannot speak. Perhaps this one was possessed by a spirit. If not, the people must have heard wrong. And yet it is said that when things are done out of season, and discontents and complaints are stirring among the people, then speechless things do speak."

Human Sacrifices.--Human sacrifices appear to have been not altogether unknown. The *Commentary* tells us that in B.C. 637, in consequence of a failure to appear and enter into a covenant, the Viscount of Tseng was immolated by the people of the Chu State, to appease the wild tribes of the east. The Minister of War protested: "In ancient times the six domestic animals were not offered promiscuously in sacrifice; and for small matters, the regular sacrificial animals were not used. How then should we dare to offer up a man? Sacrifices are performed for the benefit of men, who thus as it were entertain the spirits. But if men sacrifice men, who will enjoy the offering?"

Again, in B.C. 529, the ruler of the Ch'u State destroyed the Ts'ai State, and offered up the heir apparent as a victim. An officer said, "This is inauspicious. If the five sacrificial animals may not be used promiscuously, how much less can a feudal prince be offered up?"

The custom of burying live persons with the dead was first practised in China in B.C. 580. It is said to have been suggested by an earlier and more harmless custom of placing straw and wooden effigies in the mausolea of the great. When the "First Emperor" died in B.C. 210, all those among his wives who had borne no children were buried alive with him.

Praying for Rain.--From another Commentary on the *Spring and Autumn*, by Ku-liang Shu, fourth century B.C., we have the following note on Prayers for Rain, which are still offered up on occasions of drought, but now generally through the medium of Taoist and Buddhist priests:--

"Prayers for rain should be offered up in spring and summer only; not in autumn and winter. Why not in autumn and winter? Perhaps the moisture of growing things is not then exhausted; neither has man reached the limit of his skill. Why in spring and summer? Because time is pressing and man's skill is of no further avail. How so? Because without rain just then nothing could be made to grow; the crops would fail, and famine ensue. But why wait until time is pressing, and man's skill of no further avail? Because to pray for rain is the same thing as asking a favour, and the ancients did not lightly ask favours. Why so? Because they held it more blessed to give than to receive; and as the latter excludes the former, the main object of man's life is taken away. How is praying for rain asking a favour? It is a request that God will do something for us. The divine men of old who had any request to make to God were careful to prefer it in due season. At the head of all his high officers of State, the prince would proceed in person to offer up his prayer. He could not ask any one else to go as his proxy."

Posthumous Honours for Confucius.--Before leaving Confucius, it is necessary to add that now for many centuries he has been the central figure and object of a cult as sincere as ever offered by man to any being, human or divine. The ruler of Confucius' native State of Lu was profoundly distressed by the Sage's death, and is said to have built a shrine to commemorate his great worth, at which sacrifices were offered at the four seasons. By the time however that the Chou dynasty was drawing to its close (third century B.C.), it would be safe to say that, owing to civil war and the great political upheaval generally, the worship of Confucius was altogether discontinued. It certainly did not flourish under the "First Emperor" (see *post*), and was only revived in B.C. 195 by the first Emperor of the Han dynasty, who visited the grave of Confucius in Shantung and sacrificed to his spirit a pig, a sheep, and an ox. Fifty years later a temple was built to Confucius at his native place; and in A.D. 72 his seventy-two disciples were admitted to share in the worship, music being shortly afterwards added to the ceremonial. Gradually, the people came to look upon Confucius as a god, and women used to pray to him for children, until the practice was stopped by Edict in A.D. 472. In 505, which some consider to be the date of the first genuine Confucian Temple, wooden images of the Sage were introduced; in 1530 these were abolished, and inscribed tablets of wood, in use at the present day, were substituted. In 555 temples were placed in all prefectural cities; and later on, in all the important cities and towns of the empire. In the second and eighth months of each year, before dawn, sacrifices to Confucius are still celebrated with considerable solemnity and pomp, including music and dances by bands of either thirty-six or sixty-four performers.

Mencius and Confucianism.--Mencius, who lived B.C. 372-289, and devoted himself to the task of spreading and consolidating the Confucian teachings, made no attempt to lead back the Chinese people towards their early beliefs in a personal God and in a spiritual world beyond the ken of mortals. He observes in a general way that "those who obey God are saved, while those who rebel against Him perish," but his reference is to this life, and not to a future one. He also says that those whom God destines for some great part, He first chastens by suffering and toil. But perhaps his most original contribution will be found in the following paragraph:--

"By exerting his mental powers to the full, man comes to understand his own nature. When he understands his own nature, he understands God."

In all the above instances the term used for God is *T'ien*. Only in one single passage does Mencius use *Shang Ti*:--"Though a man be wicked, if he duly prepares himself by fasting and abstinence and purification by water, he may sacrifice to God."

Ch'u Yuan.--The statesman-poet Ch'u Yuan, B.C. 332-295, who drowned himself in despair at his country's outlook, and whose body is still searched for annually at the Dragon-Boat festival, frequently alludes to a Supreme Being:--

Almighty God, Thou who art impartial,
And dost appoint the virtuous among men as Thy Assistants.

One of his poems is entitled "God Questions," and consists of a number of questions on various mysteries in the universe. The meaning of the title would be better expressed by "Questions put to God," but we are told that such a phrase was impossible on account of the holiness of God and the irreverence of questioning Him. One question was, "Who has handed down to us an account of the beginning of all things, and how do we know anything about the time when heaven and earth were without form?" Another question was, "As Nu-ch'i had no husband, how could she bear nine sons?" The *Commentary* tells us that Nu-ch'i was a "divine maiden," but nothing more seems to be known about her.

The following prose passage is taken from Ch'u Yuan's biography:--

"Man came originally from God, just as the individual comes from his parents. When his span is at an end, he goes back to that from which he sprang. Thus it is that in the hour of bitter trial and exhaustion, there is no man but calls to God, just as in his hours of sickness and sorrow every one of us will turn to his parents."

The great sacrifices to God and to Earth, as performed by the early rulers of China, had been traditionally associated with Mount T'ai, in the modern province of Shantung, one of China's five sacred mountains. Accordingly, in B.C. 219, the self-styled "First Emperor," desirous of restoring the old custom, which had already fallen into desuetude, proceeded to the summit of Mount T'ai, where he is said to have carried out his purpose, though what actually took place was always kept a profound secret. The literati, however, whom the First Emperor had persecuted by forbidding any further study of the Confucian Canon, and burning all the copies he could lay hands on, gave out that he had been prevented from performing the sacrifices by a violent storm of rain, alleging as a reason that he was altogether deficient in the virtue required for such a ceremony.

It may be added that in B.C. 110 the then reigning Emperor proceeded to the summit of Mount T'ai, and performed the great sacrifice to God, following this up by sacrificing to Earth on a hill at the foot of the mountain. At the ceremony he was dressed in yellow robes, and was accompanied by music. During the night there was light, and a white cloud hung over the altar. The Emperor himself declared that he saw a dazzling glory, and heard a voice speaking to him. The truthful historian--the Herodotus of China--who has left an account of these proceedings, accompanied the Emperor on this and other occasions; he was also present at the sacrifices offered before the departure of the mission, and has left it on record that he himself actually heard the voices of spirits.

CHAPTER III

TAOISM

Lao Tzu.--Meanwhile, other influences had been helping to divert the attention of the Chinese people from the simple worship of God and of the powers of nature. The philosophy associated with the name of Lao Tzu, who lived nobody knows when,--probably about B.C. 600--which is popularly known as Taoism, from Tao, the omnipresent, omnipotent, and unthinkable principle on which it is based, operated with Confucianism, though in an opposite direction, in dislimning the old faith while putting nothing satisfactory in its place. Confucianism, with its shadowy monotheistic background, was at any rate a practical system for everyday use, and it may be said to contain all the great ethical truths to be found in the teachings of Christ. Lao Tzu harped upon a doctrine of Inaction, by virtue of which all things were to be accomplished,--a perpetual accommodation of self to one's surroundings, with the minimum of effort, all progress being spontaneous and in the line of least resistance. Such a system was naturally far better fitted for the study, where in fact it has always remained, than for use in ordinary life.

In one of the few genuine utterances of Lao Tzu which have survived the wreck of time, we find an allusion to a spiritual world. Unfortunately, it is impossible to say exactly what the passage means. According to Han Fei (died B.C. 233), who wrote several chapters to elucidate the sayings of Lao Tzu, the following is the correct interpretation:--

"Govern a great nation as you would cook a small fish (i.e. do not overdo it).

"If the empire is governed according to Tao, evil spirits will not be worshipped as good ones.

"If evil spirits are not worshipped as good ones, good ones will do no injury. Neither will the Sages injure the people. Each will not injure the other. And if neither injures the other, then there will be mutual profit."

The latter portion is explained by another commentator as follows:--

"Spirits do not hurt the natural. If people are natural, spirits have no means of manifesting themselves; and if spirits do not manifest themselves, we are not conscious of their existence as such. Likewise, if we are not conscious of the existence of spirits as such, we must be equally unconscious of the existence of inspired teachers as such; and to be unconscious of the existence of spirits and of inspired teachers is the very essence of Tao."

Adumbrations of Heracleitus.--In the hands of Lao Tzu's more immediate followers, Tao became the Absolute, the First Cause, and finally One in whose obliterating unity all seemingly opposed conditions of time and space were indistinguishably blended. This One, the source of human life, was placed beyond the limits of our visible universe; and in order for human life to return thither at death and to enjoy immortality, it was only necessary to refine away corporeal grossness according to the doctrines of Lao Tzu. Later on, this One came to be regarded as a fixed point of dazzling luminosity, in remote ether, around which circled for ever and ever, in the supremest glory of motion, the souls of those who had successfully passed through the ordeal of life, and who had left the slough of humanity behind them.

The final state is best described by a poet of the ninth century A.D.:--

Like a whirling water-wheel,
Like rolling pearls,--
Yet how are these worthy to be named?
They are but illustrations for fools.
There is the mighty axis of Earth,
The never-resting pole of Heaven;
Let us grasp their clue,
And with them be blended in One,
Beyond the bounds of thought,
Circling for ever in the great Void,
An orbit of a thousand years,--
Yes, this is the key to my theme.

Debased Taoism.--This view naturally suggested the prolongation of earthly life by artificial means; hence the search for an elixir, carried on through many centuries by degenerate disciples of Taoism. But here we must pass on to consider some of the speculations on God, life, death, and immortality, indulged in by Taoist philosophers and others, who were not fettered, as the Confucianists were, by traditional reticence on the subject of spirits and an unseen universe.

Spirits must exist.--Mo Tzu, a philosopher of the fourth and fifth centuries B.C., was arguing one day for the existence of spirits with a disbelieving opponent. "All you have to do," he said, "is to go into any village and make enquiries. From of old until now the people have constantly seen and heard spiritual beings; how then can you say they do not exist? If they had never seen nor heard them, could people say that they existed?" "Of course," replied the disbeliever, "many people have seen and heard spirits; but is there any instance of a properly verified appearance?" Mo Tzu then told a long story of how King Hsuan, B.C. 827-781, unjustly put to death a Minister, and how the latter had said to the King, "If there is no consciousness after death, this matter will be at an end; but if there is, then within three years you will hear from me." Three years later, at a grand durbar, the Minister descended from heaven on a white horse, and shot the King dead before the eyes of all.

Traces of Mysticism.--Chuang Tzu, the famous philosopher of the third and fourth centuries B.C., and exponent of the Tao of Lao Tzu, has the following allusions to God, of course as seen through Taoist glasses:--

"God is a principle which exists by virtue of its own intrinsicality, and operates spontaneously without self-manifestation.

"He who knows what God is, and what Man is, has attained. Knowing what God is, he knows that he himself proceeded therefrom. Knowing what Man is, he rests in the knowledge of the known, waiting for the knowledge of the unknown.

"The ultimate end is God. He is manifested in the laws of nature. He is the hidden spring. At the beginning of all things, He was."

Taoism, however, does not seem to have succeeded altogether, any more than Confucianism, in altogether estranging the Chinese people from their traditions of a God, more or less personal, whose power was the real determining factor in human events. The great general Hsiang Yu, B.C. 233-202, said to his charioteer at the battle which proved fatal to his fortunes, "I have fought no fewer than seventy fights, and have gained dominion over the empire. That I am now brought to this pass is because God has deserted me."

CHAPTER IV

MATERIALISM

Yang Hsiung.--Yang Hsiung was a philosopher who flourished B.C. 53-A.D. 18. He taught that the nature of man at birth is neither good nor evil, but a mixture of both, and that development in either direction depends wholly upon environment. To one who asked about God, he replied, "What have I to do with God? Watch how without doing anything He does all things." To another who said, "Surely it is God who fashions and adorns all earthly forms," he replied, "Not so; if God in an earthly sense were to fashion and adorn all things, His strength would not be adequate to the task."

Wang Ch'ung.--Wang Ch'ung, A.D. 27-97, denies that men after death live again as spiritual beings on earth. "Animals," he argues, "do not become spirits after death; why should man alone undergo this change? . . . That which informs man at birth is vitality, and at death this vitality is extinguished. Vitality is produced by the pulsations of the blood; when these cease, vitality is extinguished, the body decays, and becomes dust. How can it become a spirit? . . . When a man dies, his soul ascends to heaven, and his bones return (*kuei*) to earth; therefore he is spoken of as a disembodied spirit (*kuei*), the latter word really meaning that which has returned. . . . Vitality becomes humanity, just as water becomes ice. The ice melts and is water again; man dies and reverts to spirituality. . . . The spirits which people see are invariably in the form of human beings, and that very fact is enough of itself to prove that these apparitions cannot be the souls of dead men. If a sack is filled with grain, it will stand up, and is obviously a sack of grain; but if the sack is burst and the grain falls out, then it collapses and disappears from view. Now, man's soul is enfolded in his body as grain in a sack. When he dies his body decays and his vitality is dissipated; and if when the grain is taken away the sack loses its form, why, when the vitality is gone, should the body obtain a new shape in which to appear again in the world? . . . The number of persons who have died since the world began, old, middle-aged, and young, must run into thousands of millions, far exceeding the number of persons alive at the present day. If every one of these has become a disembodied spirit, there must be at least one to every yard as we walk along the road; and those who die must now suddenly find themselves face to face with vast crowds of spirits, filling every house and street. . . . People say that spirits are the souls of dead men. That being the case, spirits should always appear naked, for surely it is not contended that clothes have souls as well as men. . . . It can further be shown not only that dead men never become spirits, but also that they are without consciousness, by the fact that before birth they are without consciousness. Before birth man rests in the First Cause; when he dies he goes back to the First Cause. The First Cause is vague and without form, and man's soul is there in a state of unconsciousness. At death the soul reverts to its original state: how then can it possess consciousness? . . . As a matter of fact, the universe is full of disembodied spirits, but these are not the souls of dead men. They are beings only of the mind, conjured up for the most part in sickness, when the patient is especially subject to fear. For sickness induces fear of spirits; fear of spirits causes the mind to dwell upon them; and thus apparitions are produced."

Another writer enlarges on the view that kuei "disembodied spirit" is the same as *kuei* "to return." "At death, man's soul returns to heaven, his flesh to earth, his blood to water, his blood-vessels to marshes, his voice to thunder, his motion to the wind, his sleep to the sun and moon, his bones to trees, his muscles to hills, his teeth to stones, his fat to dew, his hair to grass, while his breath returns to man."

Attributes of God.--There was a certain philosopher, named Ch'in Mi (died A.D. 226), whose services were much required by the King of Wu, who sent an envoy to fetch him. The envoy took upon himself to catechise the philosopher, with the following result:--

"You are engaged in study, are you not?" asked the envoy.

"Any slip of a boy may be that," replied Ch'in; "why not I?"

"Has God a head?" said the envoy.

"He has," was the reply.

"Where is He?" was the next question.

"In the West. The *Odes* say,

He gazed fondly on the West,

From which it may be inferred that his head was in the West."

"Has God got ears?"

"God sits on high," replied Ch'in, "but hears the lowly. The *Odes* say,

The crane cries in the marsh,
And its cry is heard by God.

If He had not ears, how could He hear it?"

"Has God feet?" asked the envoy.

"He has," replied Ch'in. "The Odes say,

The steps of God are difficult;
This man does not follow them.

If He had no feet, how could He step?"

"Has God a surname?" enquired the envoy. "And if so, what is it?"

"He has a surname," said Ch'in, "and it is Liu."

"How do you know that?" rejoined the other.

"The surname of the Emperor, who is the Son of Heaven, is Liu," replied Ch'in; "and that is how I know it."

These answers, we are told, came as quickly as echo after sound. A writer of the ninth century A.D., when reverence for the one God of ancient China had been to a great extent weakened by the multiplication of inferior deities, tells a story how this God, whose name was Liu, had been displaced by another God whose name was Chang.

The Hsing ying tsa lu has the following story. There was once a very poor scholar, who made it his nightly practice to burn incense and pray to God. One evening he heard a voice from above, saying, "God has been touched by your earnestness, and has sent me to ask what you require." "I wish," replied the scholar, "for clothes and food, coarse if you will, sufficient for my necessities in this life, and to be able to roam, free from care, among the mountains and streams, until I complete my allotted span; that is all." "All!" cried the voice, amid peals of laughter from the clouds. "Why, that is the happiness enjoyed by the spirits in heaven; you can't have that. Ask rather for wealth and rank."

Good and Evil.--It has already been stated that the Chinese imagination has never conceived of an Evil One, deliverance from whom might be secured by prayer. The existence of evil in the abstract has however received some attention.

Wei Tao Tzu asked Yu Li Tzu, saying, "Is it true that God loves good and hates evil?"

"It is," replied Yu.

"In that case," rejoined Wei, "goodness should abound in the Empire and evil should be scarce. Yet among birds, kites and falcons outnumber phoenixes; among beasts, wolves are many and unicorns are few;

among growing plants, thorns are many and cereals are few; among those who eat cooked food and stand erect, the wicked are many and the virtuous are few; and in none of these cases can you say that the latter are evil and the former good. Can it be possible that what man regards as evil, God regards as good, and *vice versa*? Is it that God is unable to determine the characteristics of each, and lets each follow its own bent and develop good or evil accordingly? If He allows good men to be put upon, and evil men to be a source of fear, is not this to admit that God has His likes and dislikes? From of old until now, times of misgovernment have always exceeded times of right government; and when men of principle have contended with the ignoble, the latter have usually won. Where then is God's love of good and hatred of evil?"

Yu Li Tzu had no answer to make.

The *Tan yen tsa lu* says, "If the people are contented and happy, God is at peace in His mind. When God is at peace in His mind, the two great motive Powers act in harmony."

Where is God?--The Pi ch'ou says, "The empyrean above you is not God; it is but His outward manifestation. That which remains ever fixed in man's heart and which rules over all things without cease, that is God. Alas, you earnestly seek God in the blue sky, while forgetting Him altogether in your hearts. Can you expect your prayers to be answered?"

This view--"For behold, the kingdom of God is within you," St. Luke xvii. 21,--has been brought out by the philosopher Shao Yung, A.D. 1011-1077, in the following lines:--

The heavens are still: no sound.
Where then shall God be found? . . .
Search not in distant skies;
In man's own heart He lies.

Conflict of Faiths.--Han Wen-kung, A.D. 768-824, the eminent philosopher, poet, and statesman, who suffered banishment for his opposition to the Buddhist religion, complains that, "of old there was but one faith; now there are three,"--meaning Confucianism, Buddhism, and Taoism. He thus pictures the simplicity of China's ancient kings:--

"Their clothes were of cloth or of silk. They dwelt in palaces or in ordinary houses. They ate grain and vegetables and fruit and fish and flesh. Their method was easy of comprehension: their doctrines were easily carried into practice. Hence their lives passed pleasantly away, a source of satisfaction to themselves, a source of benefit to mankind. At peace within their own hearts, they readily adapted themselves to the necessities of the family and of the State. Happy in life, they were remembered after death. Their sacrifices were grateful to the God of

Heaven, and the spirits of the departed rejoiced in the honours of ancestral worship."

His mind seems to have been open on the subject of a future state. In a lamentation on the death of a favourite nephew, he writes,

"If there is knowledge after death, this separation will be but for a little while. If there is no knowledge after death, so will this sorrow be but for a little while, and then no more sorrow for ever."

His views as to the existence of spirits on this earth are not very logical:--

"If there is whistling among the rafters, and I take a light but fail to see anything,--is that a spirit? It is not; for spirits are soundless. If there is something in the room, and I look for it but cannot see it,--is that a spirit? It is not; spirits are formless. If something brushes against me, and I grab at, but do not seize it,--is that a spirit? It is not; for if spirits are soundless and formless, how can they have substance?

"If then spirits have neither sound nor form nor substance, are they consequently non-existent? Things which have form without sound exist in nature; for instance, earth, and stones. Things which have sound without form exist in nature; for instance, wind, and thunder. Things which have both sound and form exist in nature; for instance, men, and animals. And things which have neither sound nor form also exist in nature; for instance, disembodied spirits and angels."

For his own poetical spirit, according to the funeral elegy written some two hundred and fifty years after his death, a great honour was reserved:--

Above in heaven there was no music, and God was sad,
And summoned him to his place beside the Throne.

His friend and contemporary, Liu Tsung-yuan, a poet and philosopher like himself, was tempted into the following reflections by the contemplation of a beautiful landscape which he discovered far from the beaten track:--

Is there a God? "Now, I have always had my doubts about the existence of a God; but this scene made me think He really must exist. At the same time, however, I began to wonder why He did not place it in some worthy centre of civilisation, rather than in this out-of-the-way barbarous region, where for centuries there has been no one to enjoy its beauty. And so, on the other hand, such waste of labour and incongruity of position disposed me to think that there could not be a God after all."

Letter from God.--In A.D. 1008 there was a pretended revelation from God in the form of a letter, recalling the letter from Christ on the neglect of the Sabbath mentioned by Roger of Wendover and Hoveden, contemporary chroniclers. The Emperor and his Court regarded this communication with profound awe; but a high official of the day said, "I have learnt (from the Confucian Discourses) that God does not even speak; how then should He write a letter?"

Modern Materialism.--The philosopher and commentator, Chu Hsi, A.D. 1130-1200, whose interpretations of the Confucian Canon are the only ones now officially recognised, has done more than any one since Confucius himself to disseminate a rigid materialism among his fellow-countrymen. The "God" of the Canon is explained away as an "Eternal Principle;" the phenomena of the universe are attributed to Nature, with its absurd personification so commonly met with in Western writers; and spirits generally are associated with the perfervid imaginations of sick persons and enthusiasts.

"Is consciousness dispersed after death, or does it still exist?" said an enquirer.

"It is not dispersed," replied Chu Hsi; "it is at an end. When vitality comes to an end, consciousness comes to an end with it."

He got into more trouble over the verse quoted earlier,

King Wen is on high,
In glory in heaven.
His comings and his goings
Are to and from the presence of God.

"If it is asserted," he argued, "that King Wen was really in the presence of God, and that there really is such a Being as God, He certainly cannot have the form in which He is represented by the clay or wooden images in vogue. Still, as these statements were made by the Prophets of old, there must have been some foundation for them."

There is, however, a certain amount of inconsistency in his writings on the supernatural, for in another passage he says,

"When God is about to send down calamities upon us, He first raises up the hero whose genius shall finally prevail against those calamities."

Sometimes he seems to be addressing the educated Confucianist; at other times, the common herd whose weaknesses have to be taken into account.

CHAPTER V

BUDDHISM AND OTHER RELIGIONS

So early as the third century B.C., Buddhism seems to have appeared in China, though it was not until the latter part of the first century A.D. that a regular propaganda was established, and not until a century or two later still that this religion began to take a firm hold of the Chinese people. It was bitterly opposed by the Taoists, and only after the lapse of many centuries were the two doctrines able to exist side by side in peace. Each religion began early to borrow from the other. In the words of the philosopher Chu Hsi, of the twelfth century, "Buddhism stole the best features of Taoism; Taoism stole the worst features of Buddhism. It is as though one took a jewel from the other, and the loser recouped the loss with a stone."

From Buddhism the Taoists borrowed their whole scheme of temples, priests, nuns, and ritual. They drew up liturgies to resemble the Buddhist Sutras, and also prayers for the dead. They adopted the idea of a Trinity, consisting of Lao Tzu, P'an Ku, and the Ruler of the Universe; and they further appropriated the Buddhist Purgatory with all its frightful terrors and tortures after death.

Nowadays it takes an expert to distinguish between the temples and priests of the two religions, and members of both hierarchies are often simultaneously summoned by persons needing religious consolation or ceremonial of any kind.

Doubts.--In a chapter on "Doubts," by the Taoist philosopher Mou Tzu, we read,

"Some one said to Mou, The Buddhist doctrine teaches that when men die they are born again. I cannot believe this.

"When a man is at the point of death, replied Mou, his family mount upon the house-top and call to him to stay. If he is already dead, to whom do they call?

"They call his soul, said the other.

"If the soul comes back, the man lives, answered Mou; but if it does not, whither does it go?

"It becomes a disembodied spirit, was the reply.

"Precisely so, said Mou. The soul is imperishable; only the body decays, just as the stalks of corn perish, while the grain continues for ever and ever. Did not Lao Tzu say, 'The reason why I suffer so much is because I have a body'?

"But all men die whether they have found the truth or not, urged the questioner; what then is the difference between them?

"That, replied Mou, is like considering your reward before you have put in right conduct for a single day. If a man has found the truth, even though he dies, his spirit will go to heaven; if he has led an evil life his spirit will suffer everlastingly. A fool knows when a thing is done, but a wise man knows beforehand. To have found the truth and not to have found it are as unlike as gold and leather; good and evil, as black and white. How then can you ask what is the difference?"

Buddhism, which forbids the slaughter of any living creature, has wisely abstained from denouncing the sacrifice of victims at the Temple of Heaven and at the Confucian Temple. But backed by Confucianism it denounces the slaughter for food of the ox which tills the soil. Some lines of doggerel to this effect, based upon the Buddhist doctrine of the transmigration of souls and put into the mouth of an ox, have been rendered as follows:--

My murderers shall come to grief,
Along with all who relish beef;
When I'm a man and you're a cow,
I'll eat you as you eat me now.

Fire Worshippers.--Mazdeism, the religion of Zoroaster, based upon the worship of fire, and in that sense not altogether unfamiliar to the Chinese, reached China some time in the seventh century A.D. The first temple was built at Ch'ang-an, the capital, in 621, ten years after which came the famous missionary, Ho Lu the Magus. But the lease of life enjoyed by this religion was of short duration.

Islamism.--Mahometans first settled in China in the year of the Mission, A.D. 628, under Wahb-Abi-Kabcha, a maternal uncle of Mahomet, who was sent with presents to the Emperor. The first mosque was built at Canton, where, after several restorations, it still exists. There is at present a very large Mahometan community in China, chiefly in the province of Yunnan. These people carry on their worship unmolested, on the sole condition that in each mosque there shall be exhibited a small tablet with an inscription, the purport of which is recognition of allegiance to the reigning Emperor.

Nestorians.--In A.D. 631 the Nestorian Church introduced Christianity into China, under the title of "The Luminous Doctrine;" and in 636 Nestorian missionaries were allowed to settle at the capital. In 781 the famous Nestorian Tablet, with a bilingual inscription in Chinese and Syriac, was set up at Si-ngan Fu, where it still remains, and where it was discovered in 1625 by Father Semedo, long after Nestorianism had altogether disappeared, leaving not a rack behind.

Manichaeans.--In A.D. 719 an ambassador from Tokharestan arrived at the capital. He was accompanied by one Ta-mou-she, who is said to have taught the religion of the Chaldean Mani, or Manes, who died about A.D. 274. In 807 the Manichaean sect made formal application to be allowed to have recognised places of meeting; shortly after which they too disappear from history.

Judaism.--The Jews, known to the Chinese as those who "take out the sinew," from their peculiar method of preparing meat, are said by some to have reached China, and to have founded a colony in Honan, shortly after the Captivity, carrying the Pentateuch with them. Three inscriptions on stone tablets are still extant, dated 1489, 1512, and 1663, respectively. The first says the Jews came to China during the Sung dynasty; the second, during the Han dynasty; and the third, during the Chou dynasty. The first is probably the correct account. We know that the Jews built a synagogue at K'ai-feng Fu in A.D. 1164, where they were discovered by Ricci in the seventeenth century, and where, in 1850, there were still to be found traces of the old faith, now said to be completely effaced.

Christianity.--With the advent of the Jesuit Fathers in the sixteenth century, and of the Protestant missionaries, Marshman and Morrison, in 1799 and 1807 respectively, we pass gradually down to the present day, where we may well pause and look around to see what remains to the modern Chinese of their ancient faiths. It is scarcely too much to say that all idea of the early God of their forefathers has long since ceased to vivify their religious instincts, though the sacrifices to God and to Earth are still annually performed by the Emperor. Ancestor-worship, and the cult of Confucius, are probably very much what they were many hundreds of years ago; while Taoism, once a pure philosophy, is now a corrupt religion. As to alien faiths, the Buddhism of China would certainly not be recognised by the Founder of Buddhism in India; Mahometanism is fairly flourishing; Christianity is still bitterly opposed.

CHRONOLOGICAL SYLLABUS

Legendary Period (Twenty-ninth Century to Tenth Century B.C.)--P'an Ku and Creation--First Worship of Spirits--Worship of God, with incense-- Sacrifices to Mountains and Rivers--Worship of Sun, Moon, and Stars--Institution of Ancestral Worship--God enjoys music, dancing, and burnt offerings--God resents bad government--Revelation in a Dream--Anthropomorphism--Fetishism--No Devil--No Hell--Terms for God--The Character for "God" is a picture of a Man--God and Jehovah--God in the *Odes*--Hou Chi and Parthenogenesis--Superstitions and Supernatural Manifestations--Sacrifice--Ancestral Worship--Filial Piety.

Feudal Age (Tenth Century to Third Century B.C.)--The Influence of Confucianism--His Agnosticism--Weakening of Supernatural Beliefs--Consolidation of Confucianism--Human Sacrifices--Prayers for Rain--The Philosophy of Taoism--A Rival to Confucianism--But uniting to weaken the old Monotheistic Faith--Its Theory of Spirits--Modifications of Taoism--The Elixir of Life--Evidences of a Spiritual World--Mysticism.

The Empire (Third Century B.C. to modern times)--Arguments against a Spiritual World--Attributes of God--Good and Evil--Buddhism appears-- Conflict of Faiths--Struggle between Buddhism and Taoism--Taoism borrows from Buddhism and becomes a Religion--Mazdeism appears--Followed closely by Mahometanism, Nestorian Christianity, and Manichaeism--Mahometanism alone survived--Jews arrived about Eleventh Century A.D.--Chu Hsi materialised the Confucian Canon--Henceforward Agnosticism the rule for *literati*--Buddhism and Taoism (both debased) for the Masses--The Jesuits arrive in the Sixteenth Century-- Protestant Missionaries date from 1799.

SELECTED WORKS BEARING ON THE RELIGIONS OF CHINA

Religion in China. Joseph Edkins, D.D.

The Religions of China. James Legge, D.D.

The Dragon, Image and Demon, or the three Religions of China. Rev. H. C. du Bose.

Les Religions de la Chine. C. de Harbez.

The Religious System of China: Its ancient forms, evolution, history, etc. J. J. de Groot, Ph.D.

The Sacred Books of China. James Legge, D.D.

Chinese Buddhism. Joseph Edkins, D.D.

Le Shinntoisme. Michel Revon.

Made in the USA
Monee, IL
07 July 2026

56552458R00030